WE MAD CLIMB
SHAKY LADDERS

WE MAD CLIMB
SHAKY LADDERS

PAMELA SPIRO WAGNER

INTRODUCTION AND COMMENTARY BY
MARY B. O'MALLEY, MD, PHD

CavanKerry ◊ Press LTD.

Library of Congress Cataloging-in-Publication Data

Wagner, Pamela Spiro.
We mad climb shaky ladders : poems / by Pamela Spiro Wagner with
introduction and commentary by Mary B. O'Malley.
p. cm.
ISBN-13: 978-1-933880-10-5
ISBN-10: 1-933880-10-4
1. Schizophrenia--Poetry. I. O'Malley, Mary B. II. Title.

PS3623.A35635W4 2009
811'.6--dc22
2009003128

Cover art by Nancy Stahl © 2008
Author photograph by Karen Romaniello
Cover and book design by Peter Cusack

First Edition 2009
Printed in the United States of America

CavanKerry Press Ltd.
Fort Lee, New Jersey
www.cavankerrypress.org

LAUREL BOOKS
CavanKerry◦Press

We Mad Climb Shaky Ladders is the seventh title of CavanKerry's Literature of Illness imprint. LaurelBooks are fine collections of poetry and prose that explore the many poignant issues associated with confronting serious physical and/or psychological illness.

CavanKerry is grateful to the Arnold P. Gold Foundation for the Advancement of Humanism in Medicine for joining us in sponsoring this imprint. Offering LaurelBooks as teaching tools to medical schools is the result of shared concerns—humanism, community, and meeting the needs of the underserved. Together with the Gold Foundation, CavanKerry's two outreach efforts, GiftBooks and Presenting Poetry & Prose, bring complimentary books and readings to the medical community at major hospitals across the United States.

CavanKerry Press is grateful for the support it receives from the New Jersey State Council on the Arts.

DEDICATION

In the mid-1980s, not long after I first fell in love with poetry, I became acquainted with three people who would become my most cherished friends. Joe Cornelio and I met in the hospital, where we were both being treated for schizophrenia. He decided within the first few minutes of our meeting—*before* we met, actually, when he saw me stomping down the hall, cursing up a storm—that I was the "girl" for him. Since then he has stuck by my side through stew and gruel for twenty-two years.

Cy Levine introduced himself at a local folk dancing session—"I pray like that," he said, seeing my habitual rocking. Later I snuck a cigarette with his wife, Lynn. Almost from the first, Cy and Lynn treated me like another daughter, welcoming me into their lives. When things got too bad, they visited me when I was in the hospital, which was dozens of times. They weren't my parents. They didn't have to do any of this. But out of love for me, they did it anyway. For over twenty years, without once dropping the ball, there they were.

March 2009 so much has changed. Joe has ALS, Lou Gehrig's disease, and is on a ventilator residing in a nearby hospital. Although he remains upbeat and optimistic, the disease, which has robbed him of the ability to eat, breathe, move, and speak (except via an eye-gaze responsive computer), is taking its toll. Still, when he wants to celebrate, he asks me for a poem. Cy and Lynn have, without my being aware of it, become elderly. Lynn in particular suffered from the frailty of old age and passed away a year ago at the age of eighty-one. I still miss her terribly. But Cy has lost his lifelong true love. How to comfort him is the unanswerable question.

I wish I could say I always fully appreciated the love given me by Joe or Lynn and Cy. Unfortunately, I was ill a lot during those two decades and not always able to see them for who they were, or to trust them to be benign and to mean well. They may not have known my true feelings; they weren't supposed to. Much was covered up for self-protection. But all too often I was suspicious, mired in distrust and paranoia. It is only now that I have been in recovery the past couple of years that I have been able to understand

and fully appreciate them. How much I have missed, how terribly much misunderstood . . .

It is with love and gratitude and some sadness—it took me *so* long to trust them, to recognize both how much I mean to them and how much they mean to me—that I dedicate this book of poems to Joe and Cy and in memory of Lynn.

HOW TO READ A POEM: BEGINNER'S MANUAL

First, forget everything you have learned,
that poetry is difficult,
that it cannot be appreciated by the likes of you
with your high school equivalency diploma,
your steel-tipped boots,
or your white-collar misunderstandings.

Do not assume meanings hidden from you:
the best poems mean what they say and say it.

To read poetry requires only courage
enough to leap from the edge
and trust.

Treat a poem like dirt,
humus rich and heavy from the garden.
Later it will become the fat tomatoes
and golden squash piled high upon your kitchen table.

Poetry demands surrender,
language saying what is true,
doing holy things to the ordinary.

Read just one poem a day.
Someday a book of poems may open in your hands
like a daffodil offering its cup
to the sun.

When you can name five poets
without including Bob Dylan,
when you exceed your quota

and don't even notice,
close this manual.

Congratulations.
You can now read poetry.

It is far harder to kill a phantom than a reality.
—Virginia Woolf

CONTENTS

PART 3: RECOVERY

PART 4: COPING

PART 5: BEGINNING AGAIN

ACKNOWLEDGMENTS

INTRODUCTION

This book of poetry is by a poet who happens to be a patient, and I am her psychiatrist. Nine years ago I met Pam at the request of her former psychiatrist to evaluate her in my role as a sleep specialist for her sleep disorder, narcolepsy. The physician thought I could help them both understand better how to differentiate her narcolepsy symptoms of frequent, intrusive dreaming activity—vivid visual and auditory hallucinations that occur because of intense sleepiness—from the usual "voices" and other psychotic symptoms she had due to paranoid schizophrenia. I didn't know at that time that Pam would later become my psychiatric patient or that through that relationship I would learn how engaging poetry can be and how well her poems can reflect the odyssey of a mind.

At the time we first met, Pam had been affected by schizophrenia for forty years—her entire adult life and a bit more—and was doing reasonably well on just a few medications. She lived alone but had a few friends and family to connect with, and she managed to write occasional articles for magazines on the subject of her illness. Pam shared several anecdotes with me about her uncontrolled bouts of sleepiness over the years, and clearly had all the characteristics of someone with narcolepsy. But I was struck by the vivid language she used, her sense of humor, and her curiosity about her own perceptions, which is not typical for someone with schizophrenia. It was plain she had suffered many internal battles—her forearms were a mass of scars from cigarette burns—which we did not explore. Throughout her appointment she never made eye contact with me and tersely apologized as she refused to shake my hand. Articulate and thoughtful, she nevertheless insisted that "the five people," the voices she had heard since her teenage years, were real and that her fear of them was appropriate—"they menace me: I can't trust what they might do." She attributed several personal disasters to their power to bring her harm, and lived with a constant fear of more "retribution" from them.

Like many people with her illness, Pam could understand that others believed the voices she heard were products of her own mind, but to her this idea remained a relatively useless, intellectual pursuit. Pam *felt* the voices were real, and no matter how hard or how often others tried to convince her otherwise, she could not make the leap to genuinely believe they were symptoms, not threats to her being. Her paranoia, auditory hallucinations, and delusions of persecution were clearly enduring aspects of her illness that she was forced to live with, despite the medication she was taking, which she felt had made an enormous improvement in her life. She described treatment with Zyprexa as a "miracle" that had lifted a gauzy cloud of apathy and mental inertia that had engulfed her for th decades during which she was being treated with older anti-psychotic medications. Though nervous about the possibility that "Z" might be causing her to gain weight, Pam felt "reborn" with this change in her medications, as it allowed her to discover an interest in current events, in politics, in life around her that was simply not evident before.

I was struck by how unfair it seemed that someone so bright could be leveled by not one challenging chronic illness, but two. Though Pam had had classic symptoms of narcolepsy since her early twenties, she had found her diagnosis was often questioned, or misunderstood. Her suffocating and relentless need for sleep interfered with any sedentary activity before she was started on stimulant medication, but some doctors were loathe to prescribe it. Some had used it as leverage to get her to take her shots of anti-psychotic medications. However, Pam and I agreed her narcolepsy was being treated well now, and although I offered to follow her for this, it really wasn't necessary as her psychiatrist could prescribe her medication. We parted without planning to meet again.

About eight months later, I got an urgent call from Pam's psychiatrist. It seemed she had made a rather abrupt change in plans, deciding to retire early from practice, and the timing was terrible for Pam. This change came in the last months of 1999, near the end of the millennium—Y2K—and Pam had been increasingly panicked because she was sure our world was heading for disaster. Her anxiety was propelling her into escalating psychosis just as her psychiatrist was preparing to leave. Pam's usual "voices" shifted from vaguely threatening commentary on her day-to-day life to a constant narrative of impending doom, for which the voices declared Pam would be responsible. Pam's mood deteriorated after weeks of the voices' barrage, and she thought increasingly of suicide. Ultimately, as the millennium ended, Pam required psychiatric hospitalization. Her psychiatrist felt terrible about how her choice was affecting Pam, but she needed to move on. It was at this point that she asked if I would treat Pam.

Pam was hospitalized for over three months. She braced for the world to explode into disaster and instead found her inner world imploding. What I did not appreciate at the time because I still did not know her well was that Pam was much more ill, and with several strange new symptoms, than she ever had been before. In addition to all her usual symptoms, this time she developed prominent visual hallucinations and her mood became dramatically labile. She was very depressed and suicidal, but also irritable, and explosively angry at times, symptoms not typical of "just schizophrenia"; Pam appeared to me to have a mixture of schizophrenia and manic-depression. Her sister was shocked at how her behavior had changed, and kept repeating, "This isn't Pam, this isn't Pam." Noises provoked severe startling; even the sound of a door opening to Pam's room would cause her to shriek involuntarily. Other "unrelated" symptoms developed: dyslexia, a loss of taste and smell. All the changes seemed like so many scattered thoughts just complicating matters. All the while Pam was struggling to make any sense of the world post-Y2K. It took several new medications in combination to stabilize Pam's symptoms well enough for her to go home.

Over a year later it became evident from blood tests and MRI images that Pam's dramatic illness was partly due to Lyme disease infecting her brain. Pam had contracted Lyme disease from a tick bite several months before Y2K. Though she had had a rash, she had never reported it to anyone. By the time she was diagnosed, the Lyme organisms—spirochetes—had caused small erosions that showed up on an MRI as bright white patches sprinkled throughout her brain. Her thinking, her perceptions, her mood, and her memory were all affected because of these little patches. So over the course of the next several years, instead of having "simply" paranoid schizophrenia and "simply" narcolepsy, Pam had this new twist of Lyme disease in her brain that caused a host of changes to her mood, to her ability to understand and remember, and physical problems as well.

This was an enormous challenge for Pam, for her family, and as her psychiatrist, I had to find a way of treating these symptoms to allow Pam to get back to functioning. It remains a big challenge.

The book that you are about to read represents a span of two and a half decades of Pam's poetry. Pam turned to poetry after being "converted" by a friend. Though she lived for years with apathy and other manifestations of schizophrenia that dampened her creative drives, she began to write. She used poetry to explore all the facets of her life, and especially her illness in all its phases. Whether she was grossly psychotic, depressed and suicidal, in a manic torrent of ideas, recovering her balance, or just trying to cope with the problems of everyday life, Pam worked it out through poetry. This was a huge gift. Not only was it a gift for Pam to finally have an outlet for her feelings, thoughts, and ideas, which she needed to share simply because she needed to create, but it was a gift for us. The reader will appreciate, whether you have a background in psychiatry or not, that Pam's fluid words offer insights beyond the ravages of mental illness. This volume will be appreciated by anyone who has struggled with his or her mind, and by the people who care for them, but also by folks who would like to simply understand what goes on in the mind of someone like Pam. These poems inform all of us about our world's rough edges. Like her other writings, I know these poems, will touch many.

A common theme in these poems is Pam's paranoia. For the reader who has never experienced it, or seen it in others, paranoia in Pam's case is a gripping, sure sense that danger is imminent. In contrast to simple panic, paranoia combines heightened fear (anxiety) with an intense focus on the urgent feeling that someone or something is going to attack. There are several types of schizophrenia, most without symptoms of paranoia. For people with the paranoid type of schizophrenia, medication may reduce or completely alleviate the erroneous feeling. Often, as in Pam's case, the feeling never completely goes away, and is greatly exacerbated under times of stress. I have tried to help Pam many times to get reoriented when her paranoia surfaces again. We review the idea that her illness causes her brain to generate the paranoid feeling, and that this feeling must start an avalanche of thoughts to rationalize this feeling—our brains are built to explain our sensations. All her delusions originate this way: as a simple attempt to rationalize, explain, and give context to the insistent feeling of paranoia. When she is well, Pam can understand this line of logic and grasp its truth, and release herself briefly from the shroud that she is evil and the world is a threat, and all of it uncomfortable. She has had brief periods during her treatment when she could walk easily into a store, not worrying about who is there, who might be watching, and what they might be thinking. But for most of her life, Pam has had the opposite experience—she tends to be fearful that people she meets or passes by can read her mind, control her brain and all aspects of behavior through her eyes. For Pam, passing a stranger in a store may bring on the unwavering certainty that they want her to buy things she doesn't want to buy (but "has to"), and other "rules" she feels forbid her from doing this or that that she feels compelled to obey.

Essentially, the root of Pam's persistent paranoia is her struggle with the belief that she is evil. Though many people feel guilty, or have poor self-esteem, Pam has experienced a sort of pervasive blight since her symptoms emerged in adolescence; she alternates between feeling evil herself, and feeling the world is deeply menacing. As a result, she often questions whether she genuinely has the right to exist. Who knows where this idea began, but it crops up again and again in many different forms, the voices frequently telling her so. Sometimes the "evidence" that she is evil is, for instance, that someone near her has had something bad happen to them. Here grandiosity is just beneath the surface, the feeling that she can control someone else's destiny. However impaired her logic may be, the attendant feeling of responsibility leads her to search for ways to control her evilness. Pam often avoids eye contact, or uses dark sunglasses to try to filter her gaze and its effects—or the effects others have on her. In any case, this is a clear indicator of how well she is doing. On any given day if she is able to make eye contact, I know she is less paranoid, less fearful of what she might do to me or what I might do to her through our eyes meeting. The feeling of wanting to atone for this deep evil feeling is also a constant, and because of that inner compulsion to atone, to somehow make up for what she is doing to the world, she will alternately restrict her food intake so that she takes up less space and therefore is less of a weight on the world, or she will, if things get really bad, heed the voices' commands to atone for her sin by burning her flesh. Her first poem was written about this very process.

The poems in this book also touch on other aspects of Pam's illness. Some address the so-called negative symptoms of schizophrenia. The symptoms are negative because instead of her experiencing normal interest, motivation, and action, there is an absence, a paucity of thought, a lack of interest, a lack of desire, and indecision. All of these classic symptoms are still present to varying degrees in Pam even now that she is on the new medications. Certainly many readers will be familiar with symptoms of depression, with thoughts of death and suicide, and even the fragile feeling of coming back into the world before you are ready.

The book is divided into five sections. The first section "Beginnings," covers what Pam remembers from her childhood, some of the family dynamics, and her early symptoms. This section gives the reader a little glimpse of Pam's struggles with her illness on top of what she missed out on, a normal family life. The second section covers many aspects of Pam's illness. Some of the poems in this section were written while she was seriously ill, when her thoughts were grossly disorganized. Others were written later to make sense of those turbulent times. Her struggle over whether to commit suicide, what to make of her voices, and with her insistent paranoia play out again and again in the poetry. In the third section "Recovery," Pam's poems guide the reader through the issues that have been part of her recovery process. Giving up the manic phase, gliding back into a reality that she was not quite sure was hers, and finding a way to understand what had happened to her are major themes in this section. In the "Coping" section Pam's poems explore further how her illness affects encountering normal stresses: worries, relationships, physical maladies, and the day-to-day grind. This section clearly illustrates the limits Pam's illness imposes on her life and the process of acknowledging and coping with some of these losses. Many readers will find it easy to relate to Pam's efforts at negotiating everyday life with a brain that is still quite fragile. Trying to make sense of it all is a major theme across many areas of life, whether you have mental illness or not.

Pam has a special gift that has been recognized through various awards she has received for her poetry and her writing over many years. Her efforts have contributed greatly improving to the understanding of what it means to have schizophrenia, what it means to have a psychiatric illness. But more importantly, Pam writes about what it means to be human. My hope is that my added comments will simply help readers understand where these poems came in her life process so that they can reflect upon the works with a sense of the real person and the real life behind them. Enjoy.

—Mary B. O'Malley, MD, PhD

FOREWORD

What you hold in your hands is foremost a book of poetry. By that I mean it is much more than a testimony to a diagnosis or pathology or terminology. The poems emanate from the place of the poet's illness but they are resolutely poems—well-written, sensually alert, quick to turn and notice, and startlingly honest. They dwell on both sides of the equation of life and art: testifying to the powerful and tenuous links between the two and demonstrating that art is capable of holding its own regardless of circumstances. Some of those circumstances have been shattering. The sheer tenacity that it can take to write poems makes itself felt here in ways that are both uncomfortable and reassuring.

The word "mad" may conjure up notions that are either arty or primitive. Neither would apply in this case. One of the more stunning qualities of these poems is their composure, their lack of interest in histrionics. The poet's ability to examine her behavior is both edifying and harrowing. A poem such as "Offering," which speaks to the narrator's burning herself with a lighted cigarette, is remarkable in its ability to turn and turn again as it considers the behavior. The commentary that Mary B. O'Malley provides for this poem tells the reader that this was Pamela Spiro Wagner's "very first poem." One realizes that once this poem was written this poet could write any poem because she has the ability to indulge metaphor yet not let up a jot on the terror of real circumstances. Whatever else has befallen her, in her poems she seems incapable of backing down. She has that primal confidence one looks for in a poet.

What is committed to the page has its own life. These poems have that life. The commentary is by all means important and moving and informative, but the poems will call to you in that inimitable way that only poems can call. Here is a voice that cannot be duplicated and that enters into situations armed only with language. Those situations are rarely easy for any poet. Even the sparkle of a joyful moment may be daunting when one tries to put it into limpid yet forceful words. To go where these poems go testifies to the scrupulous, indomitable spirit of the poet and also to the spirit of poetry.

—Baron Wormser

1
BEGINNINGS

DR. O'MALLEY

Some of the earliest challenges come to us as children when we are tempted to explore the world with our mouths. Sensations of taste, texture, smell, are all guides to our early discoveries. This developmental stage in life is meant to teach us about limits, boundaries, and control. The essential sense of self—where do I end and where does another begin—and when or whether this self can be invaded are key lessons here. For Pam, the echoes of the fears expressed here ripple through the rest of her adult life.

EATING THE EARTH

After Tyrone, the little boy next door,
makes her eat a handful of dirt
for telling lies
about where babies come from,
her father says it will do her no harm.
You have to eat a peck of dirt
before you die, her father says.
He also says she hadn't lied:
babies do come that way.
She cries after her father
leaves the room and she sleeps
all night with the lights on.
Her father tells her other things,
that earthworms eat their own weight in dirt
every day and that their doo-doo
(he says "excrement")
fertilizes our food.
She makes a face over that
and doesn't believe him.
Besides, she says, we're people
not worms.
And we're so great, huh? he says.
Well, I'd rather be a girl than a worm.
He says nothing.
He is grown up and a doctor;
he doesn't have to worry about
being a worm.
But she does.
That night she dreams that Tyrone
dumps a jar of worms down her shirt
and that their dreadful undulations

become hers and she begins
eating dirt
and liking it,
the cool coarse grains of sand,
the spicy chips of mica,
the sweet-sour loam become her body
as she lives and breathes,
eating the darkness.

SOLO FOR TWO

In the grainy impossible flicker of old home movies
I still can't see: the woman within the child hidden
yet as urgent with life as the flame stored
in a shard of flint:
my sister, my twin . . .

                  At three, no one could tell us apart,
and even now it is difficult as the frames age us a decade
then stop suddenly midsummer the year before we turn

                        thirteen.
Our first word after "mama" was "we," which meant "I":
we weren't merely similar and separate; we were, we knew,

                  one
and the same, no more or less than identical,
the two of us occupying the same place at the same instant.
        If told, we wouldn't have believed
how our futures would diverge, as if surgically severed,
how we'd go separate ways singly, two shoes: one right,
the other with all the innate wrongness of sinister things,
awry, askew.
        I know all this now
but can hindsight and the silliness of these doting films
bring recognition of some necessity—a seed, a tumor growing?
Nothing I see in the slip of years reeling before me and gone
uncovers any inertial law that can't be
disobeyed. The map's directives are still hieroglyphs,
undecipherable . . .

      That way, mine: a path shadowed by too many failures,
three cats for my human company and the heady draught
of poetry, of madness, the two not always distinguishable . . .

                      And this way,
my sister's: psychiatrist, wife, mother, and hers another muse

equally passionate, equally demanding: the dance.
Now I am watching a recent video: my twin
gauzy in a cumulus of feathers and chiffon
shrugs off the carapace of professional dignities,
raises her arms and glides, effortlessly, onto the polished floor
as the Viennese waltz begins again.

HERE

after Pastan

Cain and Abel,
Jacob and Esau—
God gave us only one blessing
and it wasn't one to share.
When we were born, twins,
we learned to share everything
except incubator and cribs,
and we tried to share those,
scaled our bars,
wound up on the floor,
too hard to climb back in.
Now sharing is second nature
having been first
for so long. With strangers
as with friends
I have shared money,
clothes, books, my car (I
shared schizophrenia
by writing about it)
but with no one
have I shared my body
or moved with him
in the mysteries of human love
but once
and that was not with love
just curiosity
and ultimately pain . . .
We are given different blessings.
Mine is to write.
The days turn like pages.
Life scribbles and scribbles.
Come in, come in!
Let me pour you a poem.

DR. O'MALLEY

Of the next two poems, the first illustrates the tremendous ambivalence that is characteristic of schizophrenia. Here physical contact is both desired and repulsive.

In contrast to the agony and uncertainty Pam feels about her own body, the second poem conveys her sister's well-adjusted devil-may-care attitude, which she longs for.

AMBIVALENCE

Touch me. No, no, do not touch.
I mean: be careful—
if I break into a hundred pieces
like a Ming vase falling from the mantle
it will be your fault.

JUNIOR MISS

Cool as Christmas
    plump as a wish
and simonpure as cotton

you stroll the avenue
    mean in your jeans
and the boys applaud.

You toss off a shrug
    like a compliment
with a flicker of disdain

catching the whistle
    in midair and
pitching it back again.

DR. O'MALLEY

The biggest fear of many with schizophrenia is the dissolution of boundaries. Pam, like others with this illness, experiences life with fears of invasion by others or even of invading them; inanimate objects as well seem to percolate past "normal boundaries." In Pam's case, this of course is magnified by the fact that she is an identical twin, there being but a thin "placental" divide between Pam and her sister's selves, who once shared a life that is now two.

In the following poem, "Fusion," there is a line toward the end: "If I looked you in the eye I would die." This was the source of Pam's deepest fear, the delusion that through eye contact evil transpires. But who is attacking whom?

FUSION

It was a frying pan summer.
I was playing croquet by myself,
missing the wickets on purpose,
rummaging my pockets for dime-sized diversions.
It was a summer of solitaire.
I laid the cards out like soldiers.
I was in command.

Then you came out
with a mallet and a stolen voice
that seemed to rise disembodied
from the gorge of your black throat
and you challenged me to a game.

You ate me with your mosquito demands
though I, I didn't want to play with anyone!
I hid my trembling in my sleeves,
refusing to shake your hand.
I thought: this is how the Black Death was
transmitted, palm to palm, hand to hand,
a contagion like money.

You smiled the glassy grimace
practiced for boys all summer in front of a mirror.
If *I* looked you in the eye I would die.

I knew then all the sharp vowels of fear.
It was late in the afternoon
and I was frightened
when our shadows merged.

DR. O'MALLEY

Every family has some dysfunction. Pam's early memories included a sense that she and her sister, Lynnie, being inseparably linked, were self-sufficient. So much so that Pam perceives that her mother may have felt left out. The tension was palpable to her at least.

PAM

Actually, this was an exercise in thinking about how Medea's sons would have felt when their mother murdered them, and it had nothing whatsoever to do with my own mother . . .

MY MOTHER WAS MEDEA

An absurd delusion, perhaps, but
I maintain she always loved me
even as her dagger pierced my chest
and I felt my breath go black and tight.
There was much aggravation beforehand
and I had never been the easiest child.
Plus, you should understand
her own childhood had left scars.
Certainly, my father was always difficult
and stirred up trouble whenever he was around.
I knew how things had to turn out.
I was young, yes, but I knew:
early on I had presentiments of my end,
and I felt pangs for my poor mother
when I realized she would be its instrument.
I do not forgive her. Don't get me wrong:
there is nothing to forgive. Love
may mean murder more often than we know
and as soon as I understood this I lost all fear.
Even so, I admit I was not wholly brave:
I flinched when she approached,
her eyes full of such terrible love.
But I was not altogether an innocent victim—
I knew my death was necessary
to punish my father, and when the moment
arrived I stood forth and waited.
When the blade struck bone
my hand guided *her* hand.

DR. O'MALLEY

Our smallest toes provide balance and stability. The next poem suggests that Pam lost her balance in effect because her mother, through action or through neglect, "cut off her toes" and left her that way: off-balance, unbalanced, ungrounded.

The first time Pam was hospitalized for psychosis it was a sorry era in psychiatry. The doctors told Pam's parents that her illness may have been a result of her mother's poor parenting. This approach—the "schizophrenogenic" mother theory—was sanctioned by many at the time, adding the burden of grief and guilt on top of her parents' terrible sorrow for Pam.

The struggle to identify any root cause for our feelings, especially in our families, is not unique to this illness. The help "home" to safety, comfort, and healing, must have seemed a long way for the whole family.

PAM

A dream is just a dream, there is no "crutches store" on Whitney Avenue, and many of us once lived in a culture that hobbled women. In some ways we still do.

OUR MOTHERS' DAUGHTERS

I dreamed my mother cut off
my baby toes, the suturing so perfect
she left no gangrene, no scars, just a fine line
of invisible thread and four toes on each foot
instead of five. The job done, she left me
at the "crutches store" on Whitney Avenue
where I could find no crutches to fit
and so hobbled back toward home
alone and lopsided.
This is true, and she was a good mother
most of the time, which meant
that I never lacked for anything
she could buy, yet still I grew up lame,
disfigured (though not in any
noticeable way) and always with the sense
I had been abandoned before my time.

This has all been said before: our mothers
leave us, then or now, later or sooner,
and we hobble like cripples
toward the women in our lives
who can save us. Or else we limp homeward
knowing we will never make it back
before we wake up. And when we do wake up
we find we, too, are mothers, trying desperately
to save our daughters' legs
by amputating their smallest, least necessary
toes, taking the toes to save the feet
to save the legs they stand on
in a world where we ourselves
are not yet grounded.

DR. O'MALLEY

Though she was perennially "good," as Pam grew up even the normal teen angst and attempts at independence were often met with her father's rage.

PAM

I don't know that I had normal teen angst. I would not go near my father. I was afraid he would destroy me. His very aura was dangerous. He didn't understand that I was paranoid, and naturally, since neither did I, I didn't tell him what I was thinking or feeling.

BEGGAR AT THE FEAST

*"Winter rose" is a translation of rose d'hiver, the
radish, which has a lovely pink-yellow flower in the
wild.*

We've learned to hear them, haven't we,
the sounds of silence in subway graffiti,
in a Zen hand clapping,
and on the railway trestle
over the thruway, in names
we've seen a hundred times—

Tracy

Iris

!!!LEO!!!

without hearing,
which according to physicists
doesn't matter: a tree falls in the forest
and bodies vibrate—leaves,
loam, the rush of air filling the space
left behind: sound.

Thirty-five years ago,
when words came between us,
my father stopped speaking to me,
his lockjaw shunning so brutal, so righteous,
those years I still endured the holidays
I detoured my requests for salt, the gravy,
to the next person down the table,
aware of the lightning-struck air,
the dangerous thrum
his silence telegraphing: *All
visits cancelled. Stop.*

Do not come home.
Stop.

The earth sings, yes,
but not necessarily for us,
not necessarily meaning anything
we can profit by understanding,
which is what mattered yesterday
on my half-mile last lap
when I heard a father bellow
at his small daughter, the caustic scald
pumped clear through a half-open
window:
        "Listen, young lady, when I say no
I mean no. Do you hear me?"
And she, flaming up, scorched,
helpless: "I hate you! I hate you!"
as if her utterance,
like the bottlenose dolphin's,
were enough to stun, deafen, kill.

And what, finally,
of my own father's silence?
Over the relatives' gossip, from his end
of the Thanksgiving table
where we gathered together
as usual, came jokes like winter roses—
blooms for the rest of the family

but only the bite for me,
on my knees outside the family pale,
forever beyond the kingdom
and the power.

EVENING LAND

But it should be quite a sight
the going under of the evening land . . .
And I can tell you my young friend,
it is evening. It is very late.
                    —Walker Percy, *The Moviegoer*

Late in the afternoon
the older folk gather on the porch
to drink and talk
until the sun goes down,
until fireflies deck the evening
with their ephemeral jewels
and crickets scream in the long grass.
The children play and shout from tree forts
and hidden places behind the house.
Teenagers swim, naked, together,
and neck, not-quite-making-love
in the tall reeds by the river. At this hour
evening land is something no one speaks of.

I am twelve, not quite a teenager
and fearful of becoming one,
not quite a child.
I sit inside alone
and loaf my way through the summer night
glancing through photograph albums.

They are all there, the older folk,
but younger, unreal in their unlined faces,
their trim, youthful, curiously hopeful bodies.
There is one photo of my mother
holding a dripping ice cream cone at the beach.

My father, who must have taken the picture,
is laughing at her or so I imagine,
for the picture is tilted slightly
as if he shakes with mirth
while capturing the moment.
A finger has been caught on the lens,
a dark blur on the side.
My mother looks so young, so—and I admit
this without seeing it in her now—
so very beautiful. Her belly bulges
under her bathing suit: me.

There is an old Zen koan that asks:
What is your face, your true face,
before your parents gave birth to you?
And this is my question even now
as I gaze at her stomach, that sweet swelling,
and see myself as yet unborn.
I wonder if she wants me
in the picture—me, a girl—
or is she hoping
for her first son?

The adults are quiet now.
Ice settles in someone's glass, its clink comforting.
Even the children are no longer shouting
from fortress to fort, and the teenagers
are long departed to their netherworld of dance
and electric music downtown.

It is evening land all over the house.
The old clock on the wall ticks time away.
It is very late and all that is left is the going
under.

2
ILLNESS

DR. O'MALLEY

Such agony in this poem as Pam describes the process of being drawn to burn herself —forearms, forehead—with lit cigarettes. The act brings relief as the voices are "satisfied" that she has done enough to atone (for imagined sins) for now.

This was Pam's very first poem, written in 1984. The process of writing poetry helped Pam explore and explain her illness to me and to others, though not always so intentionally as here.

OFFERING

The tip of the cigarette glows and grins
                as I lower it to you,
                        unlover,
alien body.
Martian-gnarled you seek to beat me into
                being what you want.
Vague scent of scorched skin, a singed ring
                        puckering
                round ashy eye.
Now burns the tip a lambent gray, crushed,
                torch-scorching
the merciless flesh that fears not burning
as it protrudes into mindlife,
                my grief,
                my living.

Unholy flesh, you that my wish would destroy
                in one instant of
                        longing,
be gone now. The yearning-full nights
                whimpering by your
                stone-side
                        are done.
I'd sleep in peace: you burn.

DR. O'MALLEY

Pam's trips to the ER brought fears of being judged, tortured, and overwhelmed by noise and harsh treatment.

TO A REPEAT OFFENDER

It was never anything like you imagined
from a television familiarity with ERs
ORs and ICUs, never on schedule
or orderly just in the nick of time
with a touch of humor, comic relief
always ready in the wings. For one thing
there was always too much noise
and damaged bodies gave off fluids
messy, even repulsive, if you didn't know
what to expect. The many
times you were there you never got used
to the uproar, the loudspeaker,
doctors racing from cubicle to cubicle,
peripatetic police, harried nurses,
all in service to the temple of the body,
its personal soap, the one life to live
you were always so intent on throwing
away.

DR. O'MALLEY

In "Food Sentence" to eat means sin, for which Pam often feels compelled to atone. Historically Pam's voices told her that the only adequate response to her (normal) desire to eat when hungry was to burn her forearms or forehead, the larger the sin, the longer the burn.

PAM

No, no, no. "Kill and eat" were words in the Bible, and it started me writing this poem. My train of thought was, if you killed, you probably ate like a whore four times a day turning tricks. She is turned over easy like eggs "over easy" could be an omelet. Someone wags about this, about me, Wagner. I can't get to the food to eat. I have to wear two bags over my head to be presentable; that is, I'm so ugly I must not be seen. I must be pure as glass—it was hard to figure out what I wanted to say with so many thoughts racing through my head.

FOOD SENTENCE

Kill and eat
eat like a whore
four times over easy
the eggs are gone to omelet
a fat tongue wags and Wags
and the feast is under
glass, a vacuum jar
pickled in pure air.
I'm a two bag affair.
The barter is for bread,
be pure instead be true
be bloodless, be a martyr
the foot is on the other shoe.

DR. O'MALLEY

In paranoia, a person feels certain "something is going on" though the evidence does not—cannot?—greet the senses. Mere physical reality does not compete with the emotional veracity of this position. All events—real and imaginary—are blanketed by suspicion.

All the time, there is a constant monitoring for fear that danger is at every turn. This paranoia stems from a barrage of signals deep in the brain that are prelogic, even pre-verbal. Invisible blinders lead the paranoid person astray, and there is no recourse but to go on fighting.

PARANOIA

You know something is going on.
It is taking place just beyond the range
of your hearing, inside that house
on the corner needing paint and shutters,
the one with the cluttered yard
you always suspected sheltered friends
in name only. It may be in the cellar
where the radio transmitter is being built
or the satellite. A cabal of intelligence
is involved, CIA, MI6, Mossad.
It is obvious plans are being made;
didn't your boss arch his eyebrows
while passing your desk this morning,
grunt hello, rather than his usual
"Howahya?" There are veiled threats
to your life and livelihood. Someone
is always watching you, watching
and waiting for whatever is going
to happen to happen.

DR. O'MALLEY

The "simple" act of shopping becomes a course of egregious errors committed by the undeserving, foul, evil person that Pam believes she is. She's not allowed this, not good enough for that . . . all the inner self-critical voices come to life as if from others.

In the last stanza, the fear proves unrelenting. Here even the guise of this poetry vehicle can't help mask the fear.

POEM IN WHICH PARANOIA
STRIKES AT THE GROCERY STORE

You *would* choose a cart with wheels
that squeak. Your clothes are much too colorful.
The noise your clogs make
announces you with each step. Who
gave you permission to enter? No one
wants you here. They are all watching.
It is important to know
if you will splurge
on the expensive foreign grapes
or go with cheap bananas.

Behind you, watch out. She conceals herself well
but you sense her there when you turn around.
Sound floods your ears, rising like water.
You push ahead. Quick, next aisle.
A cart left crosswise!—Who?
Why? No way around.
No thought but flight.
You crash through the barricade,
race for Dairy—
She stays just one aisle behind.

If this were a poem
a lot of things could happen.
But the poem went home a long time ago.
It will not help you.
You are in the grocery store.
You believe you are being followed.
You are on your own.

DR. O'MALLEY

Pam identifies with the deep paranoid fears others have also suffered. Here she speaks to Boris Spassky, sympathetic to his need to feel safe, find the poison, the plot to kill him.

The dead flies, minute "signs" of the danger he was in, are examples of the everyday items that become carnage in the paranoid mind.

SPASSKY IN REYKJAVIK, 1972

Boris Spassky lost the world chess title to Bobby Fischer.
"Paranoia runs in {chess players'} blood."
                          —Ronald K. Siegel, *Whispers*

There were signs, of course.
The weather was perfect each day
until you left the hotel,
when storm clouds homed in.
You suffered mild but persistent headaches,
side effect of microwave
irradiation, and chemically induced
(what did the *Americans* use?)
free-floating anxiety. It was necessary,
naturally, to take scrapings, sample
air and water, X-ray your chair,
looking for devices and poisons.
Nothing found, the contest declared
aboveboard, you still had doubts, didn't you?
Ever since you found two dead flies
in the lighting above your head, you knew
your title was lost.

DR. O'MALLEY

All sorts of auditory hallucinations can occur during psychotic illness. The importance is that they all appear in a completely credible form, couched in the framework of paranoia. Voices or sounds form the ready explanation for feelings already held that "something's up."

VOICES

Static crackling, a radio tuning itself,
the squeal or echo of feedback
before the broadcast of secrets, thoughts no one should know.

In the wall today, a colony of immigrant
Japanese have taken up residence.
They speak a dialect I alone understand.

Another voice commands the household, tells me
the right and wrong way to do everything.
A pastor finds transcripts of his advice "spiritually moving."

My friend Carol tells me I am channeling, undoubtedly
an ancient spirit I met in a former life. *Brother
Luke,* I say, *you talk too much. Go away.*

Some days there is only repeated music,
singing like it has gone to my head
and broken there, a record on a spindle turning, returning.

DR. O'MALLEY

When very paranoid, Pam used a barricade and an "alarm" of dangling kitchen pots and silverware hanging in back of her apartment door to warn her when (not if!) intruders came inside.

BARRICADE

"You are a pigdog," was the only German I knew as a child.
It was a German's worst insult, so we were told.

Woke with a migraine,
throat in my throat, thinking
in German, self-hating, my only:
Du bist ein Schweinhunt!
The lubdub of pain, too much light-giving
life unwanted again and again.
Again.

Morning slashes its name across my eyes.
A door opens down the hall, the rumble
of footsteps to the chute where the garbage falls
twelve stories to earth.
No one stops.

Dangle of pots and knives goes off,
beams rigged at my door against strange enterings,
the gunshot of trespass.
I start, heart-pound lacerating darkness,
starburst, shards, coruscations:
Who's there?
Is someone there!

Silence inserts its scarring blade.
No one, *no one*, is listening anywhere
my meager thoughts left standing, charred knobs
of trees, stubby teeth along a past wall
of fire.

Who is there?
My door is open.
Will you not come in?

DR. O'MALLEY

Though titled "Acrophobia," the next poem is less about the fear of heights than about Pam's urge to "jump" into the abyss of the unknown, to commit suicide.

PAM

Or I could have been writing about that "imp of the perverse" that makes you want to jump off the cliff even when you know you shouldn't . . .

ACROPHOBIA

It's no secret you long
to fall, don't you, through all
that blue breathless air,
want the kind of danger that is
taken in like food, though
your weight is pinning you,
the flesh of your shadow
is too tethered to earth.
You want most what you fear
most, to be taken, ravished, pushed
over the brink, your toes
clutching the loose clods,
afraid you're going somewhere
without them. But high is the same
as deep; no place for indecision.
Jump! your imp implores, your true
self, knowing you risk everything
to bank on something
to break your fall—a granite outcrop
precarious cliff-clinging vines
all the hackneyed nick-of-time ways
of slowing your descent.
Instead, earth's uncertain gravity
anchoring your feet,
you reach upwards,
to claw the clouds and sun.

DR. O'MALLEY

Pam's worst decompensation occurred in the setting of "Y2K." Though the world kept on, Pam was stuck for months on a hospital ward.

PAM

At the turn of the millennium, what I considered my Y2K meltdown, I had an experience I thought was in fact the start of WWIII. I wrote this particular poem at another time, however, when I could calmly reassess the notion that the end of the world (1 had not come and (2 probably would not come anytime soon.

TO THOSE WHO BELIEVE WE ARE
LIVING IN THE LAST DAYS, I SAY

it goes with the territory—end
of the millennium, end of the world.
Criswell promised a black rainbow,
perfect symbol against thinking we would live
forever. In the year 999, the faithful,
journeying east towards Jerusalem,
unprovisioned, starved to death en route,
and in 1900 in Kargopol, Russia,
cultists locked themselves in their houses
and set them on fire, believing God
had promised them glory. The future
scares us silly, so we do silly things,
like the farmer who led seven
white-robed cows to the final hilltop
because heaven was a "long trip and the kids
will want milk." Armageddon?
This morning a V of geese
wheeled overhead, snowplowing
through a climb of clouds, drawn home
by the miracle we call instinct,
as if the earth has a mind of its own,
and nothing human or divine can loose
the boulders of its bones
before its own sweet time.

DR. O'MALLEY

The next poem speaks for itself. Mania feels heady, immortal, invincible, powerful. Its loss or end can be intensely traumatic as the experience expands the identity of self to fantastical realms.

MANIC-DEPRESSIVE

—for Fran

Mania: "a form of psychosis characterized by exalted feelings,
delusions of grandeur, {and} elevation of mood."

Afterwards, you feel a loss
like an amputee the morning after the operation
or a newly declawed cat discovering with horror
it can no longer climb trees.
The loss is not all bad. You know, of course,
that you are whole, you try to count
your blessings on your body: ten fingers,
two eyes, also two legs
and a functioning set of organ systems.
As if this should console you!
You preoccupy yourself with it, trying
to restore what is gone,
as if joy were organic and capable
of continued self-regeneration,
a kind of emotional planaria.
But joy is not forever banished. What you lost,
that "inordinate elation,"
that sense of God, even that sense
that you yourself were God—
that, the doctors tell you, will not do
and must be treated, medicated, controlled
as insulin controls diabetes.
And so they put you on Lithium,
which leaves you bereft
of a world where magic really worked,
where God broke his eternal silence

and you, you could do anything—
clawless climb trees,
dance on your stumps,
even fly without wings.

CADUCEUS

Listen!
My silences are telepathic

like shells reflecting the roar,
the orgy of my thoughts.

Do not say, "I understand you."
Man, your mercies are my greatest fear.

I live under a sentence of life.
They are listening. Who?

Don't you hear them? Snakes, snakes,
they curl and twine,

a violent caduceus. They devour
themselves, me, my mind,

my thoughts, my eyes. Violence!
The symbol of your profession.

And a lesson to me, a message.
I am the otherwise

silence, the white space between the
mouths. Gripping

and biting, they swallow me in one
dark gobble of time.

DR. O'MALLEY

Pam wrote the next three poems during the heights of psychosis. Each demonstrates aspects of her illness: how words got scrambled and fears flooded her brain causing literal "brain pain."

PAM

I did not want to publish these three, which I do not consider "poems" at all, or if poetry then exceedingly bad poetry. However, Dr. O convinced me that they are part of my story, part of my history, and certainly part of my illness, and thus deserve a voice here.

ON RADIO WAVES AND ME, MYSELF, AND I

There is a box in my head from
Black holes studied in the physics lab of
$E=MC^2$ speed and singularities radioactivity
In lamps electric with palms touch the sole
Of the universal secret who knows where quasars
Spew out my box in brains. The box on the wall
Beams out into inner of which scissors razors.
The Navy laid out on the red carpet from the physicist armies
And marines bomb us from star wars on the
Beach when tornadoes of water being today
is S the ending the cuenta is finished tonight
of grey brutish British gray crinkled paper
cosmic intelligentsia too much for me and I am
sick of wasp egg trouble and being black holes.

THE LONG AND SHORT OF THE SWISS

The rads sound cosmic, gamma as violet sunshine,
a Roy or just Red. With the Leroi of a child's ballad,

Generation X gorges on a toxin of bodies, highway pizza.
Touch-me-not, impatient, nor the exploding of my
brain's capsulated electric charge: Grey Crinkled Paper.
Survivors will be prosecuted consecutively, A through Z.

Not Rob but Bob, who hates pear-shaped Nacirema's
out-of-kilter filter and sees too much. Discombobulated

as Wall Street and needing sunglasses, I am blind. Wishing
in the snow blow, guilty of a frame's square inch while

the prower kleg skates circular: It will still kill the will.

VERDICT: GUILTY OF A PULSE or THE SCARLETT, A FRENCH LETTER STORY

Con men don't use condoms.
They sew nine stitches running
over and over. Rats live after the
Evil Dog is dead and I am
the curds and wayward daughter
of fame and physics, endo-
and mesomorphic rock of ages
in the cradle of kittens, Shake-
speare's awful brats puking
away fathermotherlove into
their faces. I could never say
or mean to be me but who you—
they—decreed me to be or not
to be, not wanted alive or
carrion. Carry on, just a unit/dollar/
pound senseless worthless fine for
overdue books or double
bound feet parked and stood
against the law of their wish
and in a man's world: me, girl,
a failed phallic Alice without
a degree of fame or acclaim
to reclaim my Virgin Marry.

GRANDIOSE

He says:
I was always more important than you thought
with your cutting-me-down-to-size quarrel
about just who I thought I was. *I thought I was*
with my long dark hair and beard and rough
working clothes John the Baptist, prophet of God
wild man of the wilderness and would have
to preach the word of a savior I didn't quite
believe in. I mentioned my conviction to a friend
who told me to make friends with a mirror,
discover which John I really reincarnated. Lo,
I looked and saw the more famous than Jesus
John staring with his small important eyes
behind his too small eyeglasses at me staring
into the mirror at myself, yes, I wrote the songs
you grew up on: *Yesterday*, *Give Peace a Chance*,
Eleanor Rigby— yes, I was the one you swooned
over and screamed for, yet now you only shriek
at me, taking me down from a peg on the wall.
Why do you yell, Get lost, baby? *Imagine all the people*
who would rejoice to see me live once more.

DR. O'MALLEY

The random feels not so random to the person in the midst of disorganized thought. Important meaning melts into mental chaos, but each word still carries a feeling of deep impact.

"Everything means . . . " What is interesting is again that the emotions carry the words. Meaning comes first and meaning continues despite the fact that words fail.

WORD SALAD

*"Word salad," a term used for the completely disjointed,
incomprehensible language sometimes seen in schizophrenia*

Unpinned, words scatter, moths in the night.
The sense of things loses hold, demurs.
Everything *means*. Numbers soldier
with colors and directions, four by four
in a pinwheel: this is the secret wisdom.
I inscribe it on sacred sheets of paper.
The Oxford dictionary holds not a candle.
The self reduced to a cipher, a scribble,
the Eye is all, with a Freemason's lash,
and twenty-six runic hieroglyphs to share
how a stitch in time saved the cat
and if a messy rock gathers no stones,
clams must surely be lifted higher
by the same rising boats. Why, why not throw
glass tomes at grass huts? It is a question
of propriety: grass is too dignified to lie down
before gloss. Whirligig! How to pull the center
back into the world? It would take all
the OED to recapture the moths, all Harcourt's
English Grammar to pin them again.

DR. O'MALLEY

Pam's delusions when she was very ill centered on her certainty that she needed to atone for her evil. Several times she had auditory hallucinations that goaded her into burning herself with cigarettes. The voices then upped the ante and demanded she douse herself with lighter fluid and start a conflagration, always promising her that she would not die, only bear the scars of an appropriate atonement. Hospitalization was a challenge, in part because she battled the urge to search for tools and flammable gases to fulfill this destiny —oxygen outlets and hairspray among them.

MORTAL CHOICES

Off the corridor plumed with oxygen
the blue incandescent symmetry of your tiger
burns blue behind every door,
consumes and is consumed
in pyrotechnics cold as starlight.
Hope, guttering like spent Christmas,
in votive lights it candles visible death:
the mirror measures each breath,
telegraphing the code.

Your Morse is all dots now, brief impossibilities
that punctuate the smallness of what's left:
a perfect absolution, the crime
wounding your Biblical angel
on the banks of the river, flames,
those last lives
devouring the bridge to any other shore,
the last sufficient silos of breath
begging the grail of your life . . .

Here, then, is that chalice, beautiful and terrifying
that overflows and is refilled endlessly.
Ambivalent, you drain it in isolation
the stupefying liquid fire,
its beatitude scarring you, marking you
as death wakens to its task:
your perfection, cold and final as snow.

DR. O'MALLEY

The inner emotional life of someone catatonic is, of course, a mystery, for at the time you can never know. Apathy, anger, relief—all exist in this once-removed experience. But as the last line suggests, catatonia often begins when an extreme fear becomes emotional and physical paralysis.

THE CATATONIC SPEAKS

At first it seemed a good idea not to
move a muscle, to resist without
resistance. I stood still and stiller. Soon
I was the stillest object in that room.
I neither moved nor ate nor spoke.
But I was in there all the time;
I heard every word said,
saw what was done and not done.
Indifferent to making the first move,
I let them arrange my limbs, infuse
IVs, even toilet me like a doll.
Oh, their concern was so touching!
And so unnecessary. As if I needed *any*thing
but the viscosity of air that held me up.
I was sorry when they cured
me, when I had to depart that warm box,
the thick closed-in place of not-caring,
and return to the world. I would
never go back, not now. But
the Butterfly Effect says sometimes
the smallest step leads nowhere,
sometimes to global disaster. I tell you
it is enough to scare a person stiff.

DR. O'MALLEY

Pam uses a male "protagonist," but this is an experience she frequently lived with. Outward activity does not convey the ruminative self trapped inside. Again, feelings are perhaps steering the brain to endless loops of one-dimensional nostalgia or specu-lation while life marches on.

The thinking propels more thinking . . . without ever culminating in a decision. This poem captures what many schizophrenics experience: a mind-numbing barrage of thoughts despite the outward appearance of calm apathy, trapped by continuous ambivalence. No action is ever taken; the mind simply will not stop.

NO

Negative symptoms are those that represent a deficit or deficiency of something that should be present: alogia, anhedonia, avolition—no words, no pleasure, no will.

Over the frozen pond, the tree hangs empty—
no leaves, no skeletal nests, bare-knuckle branches.
The sky is gray as ice and as featureless. Beyond:
brown hills. Far houses serrate the horizon. All
this framed in the window glass he smokes by,
all day seeing none of it, mind lumbering
over and over the same slow ground, how at eight
the children called him Icky, for Ichabod,
the name sticking through high school, though
for all that no friend ever did; how one day he'd
show them: talent, awards, money, renown—
show them *something* . . . From time to time he
considers the possibility of getting to his feet,
of shouldering on a coat and venturing outside.
But thinking, thinking gets in the way
of his way and he stumbles over the planning.
Inertia directs him to another cigarette. Smokes.
Stares out the window, apparently at nothing.

DR. O'MALLEY

The poem "Too Much" speaks of "body/mind disjunctions . . . irreconcilable with the life of the body . . . " Mental illness often causes such splits. Ideas become beliefs become fears. Intangible guidelines for living make living impossible: after reading The Secret Life of Plants, *Pam, who already did not eat meat, worried that vegetables were mortal souls she had no right to eat either.*

On the other hand, at more lucid times, Pam could get grounded in the process of simply fueling her body, seeking the restorative power of sleep where the torrent of ideas and feelings cease.

TOO MUCH

For excesses of spirit
when the body walks away
without you and you
discern the auroral mist
your favorite vegetables give off
so that you can't eat
what feels too much like friends,
for body/mind disjunctions
springing you free of the world
before you've had enough,
for these and other dis-eases
irreconcilable with the life of the body:

Buy the biggest steak you can find,
the slab most resembling a body part,
and eat as much as you can, eat
until the matter of your body
matters and you think not
of the rarified ether
of higher mathematics,
but of the heavy visceral sleep
digestion demands, how what rises
needs also to fall, enthralled
by gravity and the bodily truths
flesh insists upon: that not everything
can be taken on faith,
that the world's solid facts
are all nouns that name the gore,
body and soul, all
we can ever be sure of.

3
RECOVERY

RECUPERATING

After great pain, a formal feeling comes . . .
    —Emily Dickinson

After pain's mind-numbing decibels,
in the stunned silence of an empty room
a crowd has just left, you feel formal,
you feel like you're made of glass
sitting on the edge of your chair,
fingers trembling, trying to remember
the soothing rites, the rote phrases
incanted as in a dream: *I'm fine,*
thank you, and how are you?
And still you're quivering in your stiff heart,
in all your ceremonious nerves. While
the crude ignorant world blusters by,
inside, you are just now catching your breath.
Mechanically, your feet make the rounds,
as you watch the snow piling up outside
the window, freezing the rhododendrons,
which curl against the chill.
Wrapped in winter's stupor,
the oak leaves let go.

DR. O'MALLEY

Pam wrote this about an experience she had once not long after being discharged from the hospital. She felt tremendously guilty afterward for having denied that she smoked cigarettes, but recognizing how close she was to falling back into the comforting familiarity of her own "bag lady" disguises—the sunglasses were protection—it was necessary for her survival for her to push back into her newly won recovery.

ANABASIS

An-á-ba-sis: literally "a going up"

They direction us downward,
descending, always descending
into hell, towards our primal
animal selves, those who do not know
we mad climb shaky ladders up
rarified trees, ride elevators
that terminate on suicidal rooftops—
anywhere away from all this noise
called life on earth, for what is going mad
but the self scared nearly to death
and seeking asylum
in the highest places?

Last week, I met myself on the street,
in June in a wool coat and a pair of sunglasses
over regular ones. She begged me
for a cigarette, but I had quit
recently and smugly told her I don't
smoke as if I never had and didn't
understand. She faltered, fell back a step,
turned away, mumbling imprecations.
I swallowed: a bitter saliva: guilt,
the alum of regret, but it was too
late to remember to be
kinder to the kind of mad-
dening self I used to be, the fright-
full Ophelia looking for a way out
or just another open door, the ticket
to be anywhere but here.

DR. O'MALLEY

The illness is an intoxicating experience as well as a dangerous devolving epiphany. What knowledge held in manic embrace is let loose with "return to sanity"?

Grandiosity illuminates the chaotic experience, lending an air of not only credibility but desirability to the memories she holds of the manic phase. Still, the danger of its embrace is evident too, perhaps adding to its ephemeral power.

AFTER THE FACT

Of your crack-up, the visions and voices,
after the detonation of sensible reality
to hieroglyph, malefic and fascinating
as danger always is,
after the waxen feathers melted,
after the plunge, after the kaleidoscoping
of language, reel by reel shattered,
taken up into the body
of the mother tongue and endowed
with significance beyond the cosmic egg,
after meaning is at once revealed
and encrypted, beautifully strange,
after the cipher hinging the dimensions of Babel
to the imploding knowledge of more . . .

Still you wish you could longer hold
the cup of space-time
that mysterious continuum defining life
marrying 3-D to the calculus of now . . .
and drink down that flame—

After . . . after . . . after . . .
And all lingers even so beyond the power of words,
the purpling stasis before connotation retakes hold
and the mirror repeats the visible world.
So much hangs on the alphabet's fuel,
its nutritive substrate spontaneously igniting reason
but burning and glowing just beyond reach.

DR. O'MALLEY

Many of us consciously or unconsciously look for signs that we are on the right path in life. Obviously Pam's illness plays into this tendency to an extreme. A few years ago when she was very psychotic, she agreed to a course of ECT treatment at a nearby hospital. Now, Pam has always been fearful of surrendering to unconsciousness in sleep. So the prospect of this procedure, which is done while under general anesthesia, was terrifying. Pam emerged from these treatments less psychotic and no longer suicidal, but increasingly confused and forgetful. The physician Pam entrusted herself to for this process offered a reassuring balance of honesty and experience that allowed Pam to tolerate her uncertainty. The balance of trust was ultimately broken when Pam elected to stop ECT treatments early. The challenge for Pam included finding a comfortable way to end the relationship with this physician in the midst of disappointing her.

PAM

I think the very fact that I dreamed this doctor was Medea speaks volumes about how much I trusted her, or not, which is more to the point: Medea murdered her children, for all that she may have cared for them.

WHAT TO DO WITH A DREAM

. . . of one of your doctors, the one with the electricity
in her hands, the seizure control, your brain,
the one with her parchment, her calligraphy pens
and fondness for what you would never call
even in the most polite company the F-word
but say it out all four letters naked under the sun,
a dream of someone you trusted with the frailty
of your life and the brain that has served
you adequately, though not as well as it could,
a dream that she not plays but *is* Medea, hands
sticky with her boys' rich, warm, lifeless redblood,
a dream— but is it *only* that or does it say something
more than the mind's fanciful confusion
of its female characters? You can't will yourself
to forget this collusion of identities any more
than the expert silver burglar can forget the success
of his life of crime and go chalk-line straight.
There is only one question in the back of your mind:
will she handle you with care or play out the script,
taking your life not just in her hands but with them?

DR. O'MALLEY

In the fall of 2007, Pam was hospitalized for a month and a half when she became acutely psychotic, again. Her illness became overwhelming after weeks of short-changing her sleep to write and trying to find time away from the strain of living while helping to care for her best friend Joe who has ALS. Pam was adamantly opposed to the hospital initially, certain it would be unsafe. But recognizing that the voices telling her to "atone for her sins" by self-immolation might be a problem for her to manage at home, she reluctantly agreed to be admitted. After she was turned away from several area psychiatric hospitals that were full, I was finally able to persuade an admitting psychiatrist to admit her to Hall-Brooke Hospital. Dr. Isabel Gill began to work with Pam the next day and was a tireless advocate for her recovery throughout the next several weeks.

WHAT YOU KNOW AND WHEN YOU KNOW IT

—For Isabel Gill

The mechanism of paranoia is an electrical impulse, a feeling generated in the amygdala—of fear, of certainty, which the brain instantaneously translates into a "story" that makes sense of it, the paranoid delusion.

The hippocampus, shaped something like the horseshoe for which it is named, is a brain center critical to memory.

"Whenever you feel certain a communication has a secret message or there is a secret plan or pattern to be figured out, think: paranoia."

—Carolyn S. Spiro MD, my twin and a psychiatrist

Three weeks into the five you'll spend
at the best psychiatric hospital in the state
and your treatment team, that competent octet
behind the scenes in charge of your handling and care,
still concludes your paranoia remains "incompletely resolved,"
even as those who talk behind your back talk
behind your back behind your back
scheming familiar conspiracies, which, as the team notes,
you note copiously in a nearly filled journal,
all the entries recording your amygdala's aberrant sparks
and an instant confabulation of "reasonable" fears.
Writing, you're told, is an excellent coping skill
and, if practice for your poetry, better than acting out
on impulse, or screaming.
Fourth of the five weeks, it's hard
up against the wall; you learn and forget, learn
and forget: Minds heal. Learning changes neurons.

Doubt everything you think is both "secret" and "certain."
Fifth week, another amygdalar flare, the gauntlet thrown,
red cape and quickfire, and this time you just *know*
you know. Now or never! Seize the moment and—

A light blinks on in the horseshoe of memory:
you have been here before, haven't you?
You breathe through the reflex, resist
the urge to plumb the abyss, you question
perception, question feeling, question certainty.
You do not look around you. There is nothing
to see. There are no clues. You remember
all is in fact but not as it seems.
This time you remember.

DR. O'MALLEY

The next poem explores a voice that Pam did not have as a child and still feels is beyond her authority.

POEM THAT CAN FORGET BUT
NOT FORGIVE

This poem is afraid
because I am afraid.
This poem is always cold
and shivering, making my teeth clatter
like cheap tin tableware
on a bare plate.
This poem wants to die
and be rescued too late
to regret it.

This poem has been all its life scared
and still is: scared, trembling
on the brink, trembling,
knowing the truth that lies
beyond the lies
told over and over,
though it has never been taken in.

This poem has a voice
small, smoke-rasped, hungry,
and it has much to say
about what really happened
when no one else was there
to stand to protest.

This time it wants to be heard.
This poem wants to be heard!
It will spit and curse and claw
out bejesus if it has to,
this poem means to be heard!

This poem will tattle-tale
sit back and smile smugly.
This poem will wring satisfaction's neck
and revenge will taste like chocolate.
This poem is sad as water, poor as sand.
This poem wants to live well
but it doesn't know how.

DR. O'MALLEY

This poem is fascinating because Pam has never sought a romantic relationship. Physical touch is hard for her to tolerate, let alone crave. But here she admits to interest in an experience of "first love," whether imagined or historical.

A sad and painful part of the recovery process for many with mental illness is reckoning with past moments like these. The poignancy in recognizing missed chances at a different life is certainly not unique to Pam's illness, but the ability to eloquently explore such regrets is a rare gift.

THE POET AT A SCHOOL DANCE

The young fifteen-year-old in her navy crepe
low-waisted party dress is palely
bewitched by the blind date of a black-
skinned boy not much older than she.
Stricken by one another's charms

they shirk the dance, stroll arm in arm
the darkened curving paths
between shyness and attraction. She will
recall: talk only, fingers touching
like moths in darkness, arms embracing

the fabric of each smooth back,
the slow curve of waistline into spine.
Amo, amas, amat, amamus, amatis, amant—
or in love with first love, desire
and panic commingling as the bus pouts

a grey disapproving fog, the bleating
weary refrain. The boy bends close again,
leaning in as if to snatch up a flower
with his lips. Wary—first dates, no first kisses—
but loving the moonlit gleam on his nape

she leans away, falling back
into the breathless arms of schoolgirls
just as pale who cheer her escape
from a kiss she really wanted, lips
against her mouth, dark moth upon flower,

to share his air, his skin, his scent—
and the moth, mutely closing its wings

shivers, once, then flickers off
into the darkness of the past,
another lost light on the road of her life.

REUNION

Twenty years after a quarrel
she doesn't remember
was largely my fault,
I take Amtrak to New Haven
and mistake a curly Oriental
(the same dark hair, stocky frame,
a natural wave) for the friend
I last saw in Hartford.
After the ingenious cruelties
of high school lapsed
into indifference,
blunted by time and distance,
we were still carrying
similar baggage—false starts
in college, the tedious interim
of still vivid psychiatric hospitals,
parental expectations
stringent as vinegar, threatening
to pickle us into permanent
indecision: would
we ever want from ourselves
what they did?
                    Then, as if no time
has elapsed for more than a stray
gray hair, there she is, waving
from the car window,
unchanged as a cliché, though
I can't believe I, too, am
so utterly recognizable, as if
the rifts and chasms rending
the topography of my life
were not worn outwardly,

like an ancient palimpsest
endlessly repainted, as if,
given the opportunity,
we would ever choose
to do it all again.

4
COPING

DR. O'MALLEY

The power of thought—and the fear that her thoughts have too much power—still trickles into Pam's day-to-day life. Simple events—fire trucks passing—are touch-stones for more worries.

EFFICACIOUS PRAYER

You know you shouldn't
and that it is impossible to change
yet when the sirens scream
and fire trucks go racing in the direction
of your home, you do pray—
and who doesn't?—
that if it isn't your house
it has to be someone's
but better his than yours, though for a moment
you regret the malice in your prayer
and amend it to a false alarm.
Common sense tells you
not to hope too much—
the fire is already where it is. No prayer
will change that, though you know
you should have checked the oven before
you left, doused the ashtrays with water . . .
No use now in praying—
Is your insurance paid up?
Is everyone out of the house?
You can't pray for any of these either.
The rabbis say: Do not pray
that facts are not facts.
Here there is only the fact
of your gutted house, everything you owned
incinerated. You own nothing now
only cinders, your shoes, the clothing
you wear. Now you can pray,
that much is permitted. Pray you can rebuild
from your embers.

DR. O'MALLEY

Pam lives with rampant guilt over sins not committed. She carries a feeling that she should be responsible for the safety and well-being of the world. This is grandiose but comes squarely from a sense of never being "good enough." Being exposed to others in pain often prompts added agony that perhaps she could do more. When she is ill, Pam takes it further and assigns herself blame that such things happen.

PAM

The "I" here is someone other than myself, someone, for instance, who eats tuna fish, does crosswords, and longs for human touch, and so forth; someone I imagined for the sake of writing this poem. On the other hand, I do feel inadequately "touched" by the horrors of 9/11 by virtue of not having been there . . .

MEA CULPA

—For the witnesses of 9/11/2001

I wasn't there, I'm sorry.
I would have helped if I could
but I was at home watching television,
eating a tuna fish sandwich or orange sherbet.
I was answering the phone, opening the mail.
I was still in bed, asleep.
My life is still quiet. Mostly I stay in.
I solve crossword puzzles, I read,
I play with the cat.
If I don't go out often
I do sometimes long for company.
I guess you know what that's like now—
the hunger that starts deep in your fingertips
and penetrates to your bones,
how much you can ache
for the touch of some other human being.
Ah, but here I am telling you my troubles
as if they compared to yours.
You see, that's what happens
when you haven't survived such awfulness.
I didn't feel the weight of calamity on my skin,
I didn't taste the smoke
or hear the frightened
cry. I didn't see anything
but what the cameras packaged
for my little screen.
I wasn't there. I can *never* understand.
You must accept this: you are alone
with your terrible particular knowledge.

It is yours, a burden
I cannot share
I'm sorry. *I'm sorry*—
I wasn't there.

DR. O'MALLEY

The next poem speaks to the fact that there are worries about ordinary worries too—losing memory! A few factors make Pam more likely to struggle with memory problems: ECT (shock treatments), medications, sleepiness due to narcolepsy. Small comfort.

PAM

I do hope the humor comes through here. After all, I start with an epigraph from Steve Martin!

IN MEMORIAM MEMORIAE

1) Place your car keys in your right hand.
2) With your left hand, call a friend and confirm a lunch or dinner date.
3) Hang up the phone.
4) Now look for your car keys.

—Steve Martin

It seems everyone my age is losing—
give or take five years—you name it:
track, keys, sight, hair, hearing,
or hard of it already
from concerts standing close
to hear the boom bone deep.
I am glad to report I am not
among the second wave
of deafened boomers
who died—excuse me—*dyed*
the moussed grey that's left
purple or pierced something painful
somewhere visible and appalling
just to reenter dark dens of youth's
punk and grunge, Ecstasy and oblivion . . .

Frankly, oblivion's lost all appeal. Ecstasy too.
Most of us don't want to be lost
in space or even in thought.

But we're losing the battle daily, god knows
I am, the frayed synapses sputtering,
guttering, leaving us, in the know
for decades, in the dark, fumbling

for the light switch or just a candle
to hold to what we once were.
Today, for example, I said
I "xeroxed my coffee."

It's supposed to be good
to know we're not alone,
that some aging glitterary lights
are dimming too, stars whose names,
mind you, I've plum forgotten, or others,
like John, the gland-dotted yellow flower
all the rage in boomer herbals,
herb for all that ails—today I couldn't find
that blankety-blank John-
something-or-other anywhere
to unstick it from my aphasic tongue's
incipient Alzheimer's.

But "old-timer's" disease
is the midlife crisis of baby boomers,
I'm told, so I'm not alone, which is
like saying the very elegance of the company
on board a sinking *Titanic* ought to reassure.
I said, I said I "xeroxed my coffee" the other day—
or did I tell you that? What about lunch yesterday
and "those little round green things"
I've eaten for fifty-three years unworried?
I never dreamed the day would come
I'd have to give "brussels sprouts"
a second thought.

DR. O'MALLEY

One of the sweetest turns in Pam's recovery was her reunion with her father. Many lost years of no communication, harsh words still ringing in her ears, melted as they agreed tacitly to find themselves again in the present. The specter of her father's death —he is aging and unwell—makes their rekindled relationship even more precious.

WORDS BEFORE THE PARTY

—for HMS

After a certain age, all your friends are gone
the latest one's funeral only a week ago.
Another doctor whose memorial eulogy endlessly
praised the clinician who could never keep patients
for good reason and you decide for no memorial
but a cocktail party where all who no longer are
and your new friends get drunk and have a great time
and maybe toast the "good old professor"
they never really knew, yet toast you generously.

But right now you live, so I toast with coffee,
"*l'chaim*," tell you truths you won't hear after death,
that after all is said and done, you were never god
but doctor, professor, *Dad*, was always good enough.
You weren't perfect and sometimes you were very wrong
but your mistakes could mostly be corrected
and those that couldn't could be forgiven,
if you accept forgiveness, the hardest gift.

A daughter is a gift too, not lightly thrown away.
A father one keeps in mind forever, for good or ill.
So you will not leave me, even after that cocktail party,
you will live on in my voice, my gestures
the way I point my index finger downward or arch
one eyebrow and dip my chin to ask a question,
You will live on in what you have passed on.
Still, *l'chaim*, for the time that we have, *l'chaim*.

DR. O'MALLEY

As many of us do, Pam imagines a future ending for her mother. Grief is hard to prepare for, but we try anyway, hoping to spare ourselves pain or shock.

REHEARSAL

Preparing for loss, I kill my mother
in dreams, in poems. Sometimes
it's quick—like turning off a light

in a house I haven't come
home to in years or a sudden chime
of the bell, a stranger at the door

bringing news of something
terrible that has happened far away
to someone I always loved:

heartburst, car wreck, the stroke
that takes her dazzled, going
out with a pyrotechnic bang.

But sometimes only the slow reel
will do, unspooling a melodrama
of pallor and white sheets

and sickroom roses—
the painless unraveling
the patient good-bye.

DR. O'MALLEY

Pam wrote this poem years before her younger sister was diagnosed with breast cancer. She doesn't recall what inspired this poem originally, but likely it helped her reckon with how arbitrary and fateful our health seems. Because her sister fell ill, Pam feels the poem was "astoundingly and horribly prescient. I wish it hadn't been. I feel as if I made it {her sister's illness} happen." Her sister survives.

SPELLING BEE

Just when you're finally ready
for the complicated enunciations of midlife,
the stern orthography of your genes asserts itself:
your mother's dimples, the family myopia—
breast cancer, which killed your friend
at forty, and it's down to just you still standing
and the tumor, winner-take-all, spelling out
the dire polysyllabics of mortality:
C-A-R-C-I-N-O-M-A, carcinoma, you recite,
as alphabets of chemo zap friendly cells
along with the rogue typos of malignancy.
But here, this is still your first draft.
Survival's phonetic, so you sound it out,
determined to have the last word.

DR. O'MALLEY

Pam regrets that her illness limits what she can offer her friend Joe, who has amy-otrophic lateral sclerosis (ALS), or Lou Gehrig's disease. She strains to discern the subtle losses in his strength, fearing his death. Distressing as it is to hear him struggle to breathe on a ventilator, she remains at his side, fighting to get him good care, hold-ing his hand in comfort although the touch is never comfortable for her. All the worry, all the angst is multiplied by her brain's sensitivity. Still, she is there.

PAM

I wrote this before Joe was on the ventilator, when he could still walk and talk and eat, when I still had to worry he might fall or choke on food. I wish I still had such worries!

LOU GEHRIG'S MAN

Both schizophrenic, you watch his every move
being awkward, clumsy, for signs of slowing,
weakness the cardinal symptom of the second hand
he's been handed at the too young middle age
of fifty, fearful of choking episodes and falls,

of losses unprepared for in any unexpected absence
at a time when he for once needs you most,
wanting no shoe to drop that you can't catch
and retie, desperate to keep him this side
of where the doctors say such illness "invariably"

leads, the good night he won't join gentle.
But your own illness, that hand, is too much
in the way in such ways that interfere
and intersect with the care you wish
you could give: the casual touch that still feels

invasive given, received, is swallowed but festers;
the unforgotten trauma of suctioned mucus
and uncontrollable coughing. If only
you were a different person you would be
a different person and more capable, happy to

do it all. Now all you want to do is catch the second shoe.
For he is Huck, unquenchably on meds content,
unable to look at living and see blues,
ruined choirs of hope, broken wishes, tragedy—
no, it all interests, all of it a source, a font

to fascinate the mind, as well as eyes and ears,
which he says are enough to tether him

when his body, unmoored from brain,
paralyzed, no longer moves a muscle.
His mind is rich and teeming as a city,

still ravenous to know what's up and coming
in the mobile world that would move past him,
but for his drive to counterclockwise time,
to dip his hands into a flowing stream
and cup the future in his palms.

PAM

I wrote the next three-part poem about one of the very few friends I had in high school. Note: If two pictures were taken and superimposed, the way you occasionally used to get two ghostly images on a film photograph, you might see one image of a person rising from bed with another image of a person lying down. Hence the reference to two ghosts, one rising and one "napping," that is, dead.

DR. O'MALLEY

I would add that Pam remained, her "ghost" napping in real life due to narcolepsy, while Susie's ghost rose out of her dead body.

THREE, FOR THOSE LEFT BEHIND

1. *Grieving and Staying*

The dead do not need us
to grieve or tear our hair
or keen extravagantly.
Stepping free of flesh
a double exposure (one ghost
rising from bed, another napping
at midday), their spirits follow
the curves of their late bodies,
rehearsing again and again
what we're always too late for.
Just so, my friend Susie,
scrubbed clean of life's debris,
twenty years later returning
in my dream of the dead
returning and I can't let go
my guilty retrospection,
the arrogant suspicion
I could have saved her.
Now, though I know no dream
will return her utterly, I cling
to this one: Susie and I at twenty-one
standing before two doors,
how she points me towards the one
where a celebration is taking place
then disappears through the other
marked No Exit, as if it has to be,
as if it's fair, as if either
of us in this world
has ever had a choice.

2. At the Lake, Under the Moon

In memory, the moon's always a new dime,
glinting off the dark chop, ticking the night away

ruthless and indifferent as a parking meter.
As always, the lake shimmers, ebony splashed

with silver and we're sitting there at the end
of the dock, thirteen, dangling our bare feet

above the water's coruscating skin. We barely
ruffle the surface but it's enough

to shatter the still shaft of moonglow,
potsherds of mercury, dancing tesserae, a mosaic

of light illuminating the water.
Is it possible we don't yet suspect

how things must turn out? We shed our clothes
to swim shy and bare-skinned, silvered bubbles

rising to the surface like stars
of the wayward constellations

by which we'll navigate our separate lives.
What we know is this: the sleek water

rolling off our skin, the frangible sand, schools of
glowing nightfish nosing amid algae.

We can't guess how fate will interpose
its coups and tragedies, how far in ten years

we will have traveled from that night.
I never got to say good-bye.

I scatter your white ashes,
moonlight over dark water.

3. *In My Dreams You Are Not Silent*

Time heals nothing
but the space left behind
is filled, little by little,
with the critical minutiae
that make a life: shirts
at the cleaners, supper
in its pots, a half-read book
overdue at the library,
lying open, facedown,
on the table.

DR. O'MALLEY

The next poem reveals a friendship lost but also the birth of Pam's conversion to poetry.

YOU WERE A POET ONCE

You were a poet once. You touched my soul
with the gift of poems, teaching me to read and write—
oh, inevitably to write them, for writing made me whole
and I could never *not* write. I had no special goal,
only to "pour out a poem" and work it right.

That took me years. I was such a fool—
dreamy cups of poems, quote unquote, only wasted good ink . . .
But I was speaking of you. You gave me the tools
to teach myself; you should have returned to school.
You found vodka: you could not, after one drink,

stop. And though it seemed deliberate, a choice,
I suppose you couldn't help it. On conversion day
you recited Hopkins's "Spring and Fall," your voice
for once not blurred by Popov. (Still, I didn't dare rejoice.)
You were so sure, so caught up in what you had to say.

It changed me utterly. Few experiences work such magic.
Why you quit poetry for drink I'll never understand.
Life made you querulously unhappy, so there's a logic
in your refusal to live. But I'll never not think it tragic
how your gift to me soured in your own hands.

POEM

You ask me in anger
to write about anger,
the hot flare of it, the cold steel
as we almost come to blows
and each word blisters my fingers
as I take out my wrath
at the typewriter.

Later you are calmer
and in silence do not so much
ask for forgiveness—we both were wrong—
as ask for a poem.

Here it is, love,
here it is.

POEM WRITTEN WHILE THE REFRIGERATOR DEFROSTS

and autumn throws its frail bones about the house
and the phone is silent all day.
This poem breaks out of nowhere
under the feeble old torture
of water drip dripping without rhythm,
without pattern, into a stained aluminum turkey pan
that has seen better days and all of them holidays.

I imagine callers, visitors, wrong numbers
struck into conversation
by husky male voices, men who must be
beautiful they are so welcome.
I tell them I am a poet.
I do not tell them I write only when lonely
or when the rotten ice drips softly into a pan.
I tell them all the secrets I've been sworn to
and I tell them jokes
just to hear the fine solid sound
of their laughter. I tell them my name
is Mabel Fitzwillow or Phoebe Sparrow.
I am, of course, too old for them
but they need not know it.
When I'm in a good mood I tell them
my aunt was Sarah Bernhardt,
that I, too, am a famous actress
though *both* my legs are wood
and I have a terrible memory.
I do not recall everything they tell me.
Their stories vary and are not all pleasant.
But once I talked for two hours
with a man whose lover was his own sister.

His voice was sweet, gentle. He told me
he loved his sister more than any other
woman he'd ever met. When we said good-bye
he asked if he might call again—he had
the number—might meet, buy me coffee downtown
or take me to lunch at noon.

No—the truth is that no one calls, no one
visits. All day long the ice melts into the turkey pan.
I write lonely poems of the worst sort
and set each one ablaze on the stove.
By nightfall the ice is gone, the pan full of frost-bitter water.
Carefully I drain it into the sink.
The pan is cold, flocked with bits of ice
and dead insects. I wipe away the grime,
dry all surfaces, then turn the power on once more
and close the door.

DR. O'MALLEY

Pam knows she gets suckered. When her illness was not as well managed, she had less insight into others and was frequently a target for others' greedy plans. Though better now, Pam still finds it difficult to spot a fake friend; ironically, though paranoid, she is too trusting. Just another way the mentally ill become terribly vulnerable.

PAM

But I can also see the humor in the situation as I describe it in the poem.

WOMAN READING HER MAIL

It's not so bad, being Barnum's
born-every-second. Born but once,
I've been suckered time after time after time,
never learning even the hard way
to tell a shyster from an honest man
or to give less gullibly.
I still trust telephone charity solicitors,
the alley-cat rescue leagues
that send out those awful pictures;
I sponsor children in several countries
who don't answer my letters,
but since they are busy with the schoolwork
I am paying for, I am content.
I don't complain, not even when the FBI
cautions my name ladders high on a list
found on a sought-after scammer
who has sugared old ladies
and middle-aged me out of our accounts
for not the good cause we believed in.
Always there's my shameless delight
like that secret pleasure shared
between pretty women and voyeurs
in being taken by the con artist
all the time plucking my harp,
archangel.

DR. O'MALLEY

Pam's poetry began to get wider attention when she won the international Poetry Competition sponsored by BBC World Service in 2002. Pam wrote this poem about Nobelist John Nash, who has schizophrenia, before the movie A Beautiful Mind *immortalized him.*

THE PRAYERS OF THE MATHEMATICIAN

. . . rise without sound,
primes uttered like a rosary's
beaded polynomials of devotion,
climbing the sky towards a god
unknowable as the dark infinity
between rational and irrational
numbers. His hair in a wild corona
framing eyes so deep-set
they seem to drown what's caught there,
knowing the hardest questions
may sometimes answer,
he wanders the halls
pale and abstracted as pi,
trailing numbers in chalk dust,
like the spectral footprints of a ghost
no one remembers passing there,
these incandescents of his faith
illuminating all the unsayables
as only equations can,
in brief yellow chalk on a green board:
that life yearns towards binariness,
that our ending is in our beginning,
that if we name as nouns
the verbs he numbers in strictest silence,
our dualism's just as binary:
good or evil, pure or profane,
we only constrain what he sets free
with his meticulous 1s,
his careful and perfect 0s.

5
BEGINNING AGAIN

TO FORGIVE IS . . .

to begin
and there is so much to forgive:
for one, your parents, one and two,
out of whose dim haphazard coupling
you sprang forth roaring, indignantly alive.
For this, whatever else followed,
innocent and guilty, forgive them.
If it is day, forgive the sun
its white radiance blinding the eye;
forgive also the moon for dragging the tides,
for her secrets, her half heart of darkness;
whatever the season, forgive it its various
assaults—floods, gales, storms
of ice—and forgive its changing;
for its vanishing act, stealing what you love
and what you hate, indifferent,
forgive time; and likewise forgive
its fickle consort, memory, which fades
the photographs of all you can't remember;
forgive forgetting, which is chaste
and kinder than you know;
forgive your age and the age you were
when happiness was afire in your blood
and joy sang hymns in the trees;
forgive, too, those trees, which have died;
and forgive death for taking them,
inexorable as God; then forgive God
His terrible grandeur, His unspeakable
Name; forgive, too, the poor devil
for a celestial fall no worse than your own.
When you have forgiven whatever is of earth,
of sky, of water, whatever is named,

whatever remains nameless,
forgive, finally, your own sorry self,
clothed in temporary flesh,
the breath and blood of you
already dying.

               Dying, forgiven, now you begin.

ACKNOWLEDGMENTS

If you think a poem is difficult to write, try thanking all those who have played a role in your book or helped you along the way, and despite memory loss due to electric shock treatments, Lyme disease, and narcolepsy, do so without leaving anyone out in the process. It can't be done. I discovered that upon remembering for the third time one more person critical to my writing life just when I thought I'd thanked everyone. Which leads me to the realization that there will *always* be "just one more" VIP in my life whom I've slighted unintentionally by the sheer effort of trying to remember all of them. Keeping this in mind, you should understand that the following are only a few of the people to whom I owe my deepest gratitude:

Joan Cusack Handler and Florenz Eisman of CavanKerry Press patiently put up with my anxious e-mails and many delays due to my unique circumstances, and cheered when I finally found the right title.

M.E.H. was a friend, but also the poet whose recitation of Gerard Manley Hopkins's "Spring and Fall: To a Young Child" instantaneously and as if by a miracle converted me to poetry. Much water has sluiced down the channels since then, but I remain supremely grateful.

David Goldberg, MD, a wise and literary psychoanalyst-in-training, treated me from the late 1970s to the mid-1980s. I wrote hundreds of poems after I started in 1984 but was uncertain of their value. He pronounced them "evocative." I didn't understand what "evocative" meant exactly, but it sounded positive. He might have said any other word of praise or disparagement, but he said "evocative," a word so mysterious and charged I wanted to live up to it. Without it, who knows? But "evocative" was nourishment enough to continue writing. I cannot thank him enough.

I met Hugh Ogden, professor of English at Trinity College in Hartford, Connecticut, not long after I began writing poetry. He was the first real poet to encourage me and was responsible for my first publication—in *The Trinity Review*. For a number of years, when I was writing in darkness, Hugh's words reaching out to me in letters were sometimes my only light.

Ed Ifkovic, a poet on the English faculty at Tunxis Community College, kept publishing "my stuff" no matter where I was or how many hospitals I was sent to. I cannot say how much I appreciated him and the *Tunxis Poetry Review*, of which he was the faculty editor, for their loyalty, even when I was at my sickest.

Ann Z. Leventhal was my friend and writing partner for many years. Though the writing group we attended in the 1980s largely disbanded after a few years, Ann and I kept going as a twosome. She was tough and honest to the point of being blunt, but I appreciated the fact that I could trust her when she said she liked something not to be saying so out of mere kindness. When she offered one day the opinion that I had the makings of one of America's "minor poets," I knew she meant it as a major compliment. I don't know that these poems rise to that level, but I hope she finds them acceptable, because her opinion still matters. Thanks to Ann for friendship, for staying in touch, for insisting that I write my best and never being satisfied with less.

I can't say enough about Bill, Jennifer, Harriet O and Harriet P, Krystyna, Karen, Lisa, and all the other regulars and irregulars in my wonderful new writers' group. What terrific Tuesdays I've spent with them! Who ever thought an evening of talk about writing, with neither refreshments nor a coffee table, could be so thoroughly entrancing? They encourage me and they accept me. I couldn't ask for more.

Bill Williams, what a wonderful man of peace and loving-kindness. Like gentle water sweeping out ripples in the sand of a lonely beach, he has opened my heart as well as my mind over the past fifteen years. He is a writer, editor, and book reviewer, but oh so much more than that I cannot possibly do him justice. Suffice it to say, he is my true and trusted friend, and I love him.

Leila Raim, dear friend and the source of many conversational peak experiences, has a special place in my heart. As a poet and writer by nature, she has been a true, kind, and utterly reliable editor. Cutting through verbiage right to the core of any problem, her advice is always right on. I don't always take it, but I do always listen and consider it carefully. Thanks to her keen eye, many a piece of writing has been honed to a sharper edge, to a polish that flashes. I know she would say that thanks are unnecessary, but I offer a million, million just the same.

Joyce Marcotte, APRN, saw me through innumerable crises, caught me when the bottom fell out and I had nothing to cling to but her strength, her faith. Because of her, I survived my life. Gratitude, appreciation, and thanks are too flimsy to express my feelings. But I owe her all three and so much more than English provides words for me to say.

Marian Spiro, my mother and my greatest supporter since I was a child, forever held as her mantra "You can do anything you set your mind to." She still does. She has always believed in my ability to set the world on fire, and schizophrenia has scarcely dampened her faith in my talents. No doubt this extends to my book as well. No matter how ill I became over the years, she never lost that faith or that hope, and always, always, she cheered me on through every small success. Though it is a paltry thing compared to what she has given me, I offer my book itself as a token of gratitude and love.

Howard Spiro, my father, has gone out of his way to see that this book was the best it could be. The short space allotted here does not permit me to write all that I feel. As a physician and professional writer himself he has unstintingly shared, and my gratitude knows no bounds. His biweekly visits have been a mainstay. It is wonderful to have a father again. That is what really matters.

Irene Kitzman, MD, restored my ability to depend on others. A psychiatrist, she combined utter honesty with kindness and wisdom. She knew what my limits were and respected them, allowing me to learn that she, and thus others, could be trusted. If I never was able to make eye contact, or see what she looked like, I knew her voice and I relied on it to tell the truth. She never failed me. For that, and for a thousand other reasons, I thank her.

Carolyn Spiro is, of course, Lynnie, my twin sister, whom I trust implicitly and in whom I have complete faith . . . What do I say of someone who has never for one second doubted that my book would be published, never doubted that my poems were worthy, and always declared that I was just as good *if not better* than whoever was the poet just then being fêted. Talk about faith in me! She still thinks I'm a genius, despite all the years of failure. Lynnie is the one I send my poems to first, my first critic, my first reader. It would take volumes to write all that Lynnie is and means to me, all that she has given me and done for me. She is my buoy when I'm lost at sea, my beacon in the night. She is my hero.

For Mary B. O'Malley, MD, PhD, my ever-patient psychiatrist and sleep specialist to whom I entirely owe my sanity and my emotional well-being, I am more grateful than I could ever say. For several years she worked with me to find a perfectly titrated combination of medications. Despite my expectations to the contrary, despite my frequent refusal to take meds at all, she never gave up. She never "dumped me" in frustration or weariness or set impossible ultimatums. She just wanted to find a medication combination that would do two things: work effectively to reduce or eliminate my symptoms, and manage this with minimal side effects. When we finally met this goal, the success was beyond anything either of us had anticipated: my prognosis became suddenly hopeful and the future bright. Thanks to Dr. O's persistence, this was, if not a miracle, then something pretty damn close! Without her clinical acumen and fierce intelligence, I would not be as symptom-free as I am today. Without her compassion and trustworthiness, her endlessly patient repetition of lessons that I would learn and forget, learn and forget, without Dr. O herself, I would not be who or where I am today: in recovery, a poet and an artist, a whole person with the rest of my life ahead of me.

These poems were published in the following places, some in slightly different forms: *Tunxis Poetry Review*: "Eating the Earth" and "Poem" were among a group of poems that won first place in 1987; also, "After the Fact," "Evening Land," and "To Forgive Is . . ." in 1994; in their special edition, *Three Poets*: "Food Sentence," "Rehearsal," and "Three, for Those Left Behind" (under the title "Troika for SD"); *The Trinity Review*, Spring 1986: "Poem Written While the Refrigerator Defrosts"; *Bitterroot International Poetry Journal*, Winter 1987: "Ambivalence"; *The Connecticut Writer* 1987: "Our Mothers' Daughters." Also, "The Prayers of the Mathematician" won first place in the international Poetry Competition sponsored by BBC World Service in 2001/2, judged by Nobelist Wole Soyinke; *New Millennium Writings* (NMW) #18 awarded honorable mentions for "The Prayers of the Mathematician" and "How to Read a Poem: Beginner's Manual." *New Millennium Writings NMW* #19 gave an honorable mention for "Three, for Those Left Behind." "To Forgive Is . . ." was first seen in the memoir *Divided Minds: Twin Sisters and Their Journey Through Schizophrenia*, by Pamela Spiro Wagner and Carolyn S. Spiro, MD. Copyright 2005 by the authors and reprinted by permission of St. Martin's Press, LLC. Several poems in their early stages were published online by the *Hartford Courant* as part of a feature article in 2003.

OTHER BOOKS IN THE LAUREL BOOKS SERIES

CAVANKERRY'S MISSION

Through publishing and programming, CavanKerry Press connects communities of writers with communities of readers. We publish poetry that reaches from the page to include the reader, by the finest new and established contemporary writers. Our programming brings our books and our poets to people where they live, cultivating new audiences and nourishing established ones.